Billboards of the Past

Randy & Sharon
Littlefield

4880 Lower Valley Road, Atglen, PA 19310 USA

Acknowledgments

I would like to thank my wife Sharon for helping me prepare this book, my son David for organizing my web site, and my brother Michael for helping me set up my web site.

Published by Schiffer Publishing Ltd.
4880 Lower Valley Road
Atglen, PA 19310
Phone: (610) 593-1777; Fax: (610) 593-2002
E-mail: Info@schifferbooks.com

Copyright © 2006 by Randy and Sharon Littlefield
Library of Congress Control Number: 2006925340

For the largest selection of fine reference books on this and related subjects, please visit our web site at
www.schifferbooks.com
We are always looking for people to write books on new and related subjects. If you have an idea for a book please contact us at the above address.

This book may be purchased from the publisher.
Include $3.95 for shipping.
Please try your bookstore first.
You may write for a free catalog.

Designed by Mark David Bowyer
Type set in Airstream / Korinna BT

ISBN: 0-7643-2480-2
Printed in China
1 2 3 4

In Europe, Schiffer books are distributed by
Bushwood Books
6 Marksbury Ave.
Kew Gardens
Surrey TW9 4JF England
Phone: 44 (0) 20 8392-8585; Fax: 44 (0) 20 8392-9876
E-mail: info@bushwoodbooks.co.uk
Website: www.bushwoodbooks.co.uk
Free postage in the U.K., Europe; air mail at cost.

Contents

Introduction
Roadside Advertising

These billboard ads were salvaged about 23 years ago from a potato cellar in Baker City, Oregon. Though most of these ads are almost 60 years old they are still in remarkable condition. Organized into 29 major categories, these ads were a unique form of roadside artwork, which appeared being displayed in many different forms around the country. It's fun and educational to go back to the decades of 1940s to the 1960s and see how styles have changed in clothing, cars, hairstyles, and advertising itself. Several ads were done in a cartoon style, while others are whimsical, and many have a wholesome appeal.

The ads featured in this book came in several pieces that I have unfolded and joined together for viewing. Though some wrinkles may be visible in a few photos, we feel they do not distract from the overall appeal.

You'll feel like you're taking a drive through the past as you view ads for Coca-Cola, Levi's, Budweiser, Richfield, Brown & Haley's, Chevrolet, and Ford, just to name a few. So sit back and enjoy the ride!

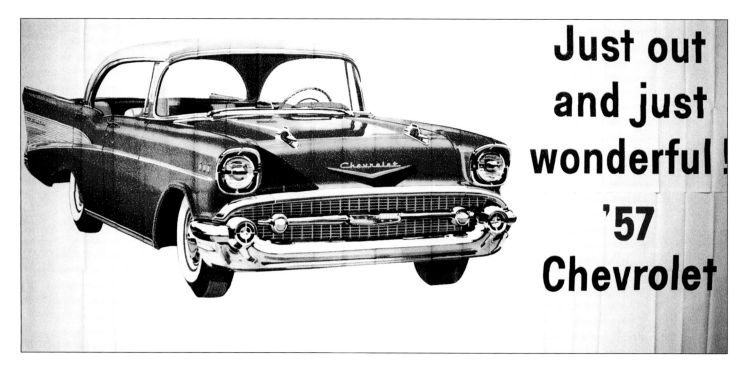

Chapter One

The Find of a Life Time

I had no idea I would be stepping into the past one day in September 1982. I had heard of some old, unused billboard ads that were for sale in Baker City, Oregon. The thought of finding some older ads pertaining to old cars peaked my interest, as I had collected old cars and antiques for several years. The owner of the billboards took me to a dimly lit potato cellar where the ads were stored. Several newer ads had already been sold as cabin insulation, but many older ads still remained. I brushed the dust off a few and saw titles such as Mercury Car/Bing Crosby, Packard Car/Famous Face, and Coca Cola/Santa Claus The signs were in two huge stacks towering above my head. As I flipped through the folded paper I could see the colors were still as vibrant and intense as the day they were printed. After deciding to purchase all the ads I moved them into storage till I could acquire adequate shelving for them. My wife Sharon and I spent several years alphabetizing and cataloging all the ads since many were still in their original metered wrappers. Over the past 17 years I have taken several hundred pictures and I still have more to take.

Advertising Agency History

Although I purchased the ads in Baker City, Oregon, from a third party, they were originally purchased by Harvey Advertising Company. During the 1940s Harvey displayed ads in small Idaho towns such as Weiser, Payette and some southeastern Oregon towns. Around 1950 Harvey Advertising moved to Baker City, Oregon, and about a year later sold out to Clark Advertising Company in Baker City. Clark Advertising hanged their signs primarily in the Oregon towns of Baker City, Burns, Enterprise, LaGrande, Nyssa, Vale, and Wallowa. In the early 1960s Clark Advertising sold out to Cosgriff Outdoor Advertising in Baker City. Sometime after 1967 the billboards were moved to the potato cellar in Baker City where I purchased them.

Billboard Dates and Sizes

These billboards date from approximately 1945-1967, with most ads from the early to mid 1950s. The billboard sizes vary. The smallest is approximately 7 feet by 19-1/2 feet; the largest is 9 feet by 22 feet, with the most common size being 8-1/2 feet by 19-1/2 feet. The ads come in a folded bundle with an average weight of 4 pounds. Each ad is comprised of an average of 12 unassembled pieces of specially treated paper, which overlap to form a single image.

Lithograph Companies and Artists

Several different lithograph companies from Idaho, California, Wisconsin, Pennsylvania, and New York designed the ads. Modern billboards from the mid-1960s were created with dot lithograph, which is composed of thousands of small dots of four basic colors. By varying the density and frequency of the dots, various colors are produced allowing for mass-production on high-speed printers. The older lithographs were hand drawn onto a specially treated paper surface. The image was then transferred to lithographic plates, one for each color. Many older lithographs are artist signed.

Most lithograph artists specialized in only one type subject matter. One of the lithograph artists on the billboards seen here is Charles Schulz, the Peanut comic strip creator, who designed a couple of ads for Ford. An artist by the last name of Hayden designed Chevrolet car ads, while Howard Scott designed for Nash. Bomar designed for Phillips 66, Morice Logan for Richfield, Jerome Razen for Shell Oil, Stu Graves for Utoco, and Shepperd for Union 76. Several Coca Cola Santa Claus billboards were designed by Haddon Sundbloom.

Chapter Two

Hints for Collectors

Billboard Categories and Pricing

In the 29 major categories of products, the most prevalent are soft drinks, beer, cars, food, and several gasoline and oil companies. The 130 subcategories contain an interesting assortment such as Coca-Cola, Chevrolet, Ford, Richfield, Wrigley's Gum, General Electric, Olympia Beer, Nucoa, and Brown & Haley, to name just a few.

Pricing of these ads is based on the style of art work, the product being advertised, and the age and condition of the ad. Prices range from $50-3,000. Ads with movie stars are understandably the most expensive. Examples of celebrity ads are Mercury ads featuring Jack Benny, Gene Tierney, Jane Wyman, and Betty Grable, and Chesterfield cigarettes featuring Arthur Godfrey, Ben Hogan, Joe Dimaggio, Rhonda Fleming, and Bob Hope.

Coca-Cola features Edgar Bergen and Charley McCarthy in one of their ads. Kay Kiser is featured in a Ford ad and Suzy Parker is seen in a Royal Crown Cola ad.

Photographing Billboards

Most of the billboards are over 50 years old and in nearly new condition. They have all been printed on heavy weight paper suitable for displaying. I assemble the ad by laying the pieces on the cement floor and lining up the design by the overlap marks on each piece. The billboards line up from left to right. After verifying the design is lined up straight I take a picture from an overhead camera. The billboard is then refolded back to its original size for storing on a shelf. The following 7 photos show the typical layout from start to finish.

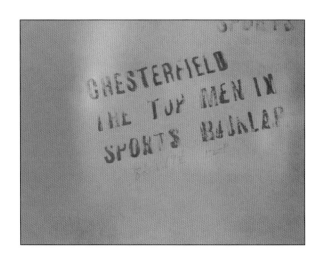

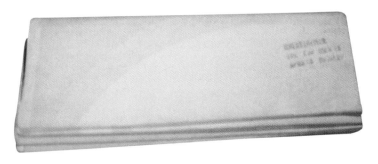

Gluing a Billboard Together

When gluing a billboard together it is also assembled from left to right. If the pieces are extremely wrinkled, most of the major wrinkles can be removed by putting the pieces under a board of sheet rock or other heavy flat object for a few weeks. Roll-on glue is applied to the over lapped areas to form a seam. I hold the seam down by putting weights on top of thin boards. This insures a solid seam. The billboard can then be attached to a frame with a heavy cardboard backing and hung on the wall. If the ad is removed from the frame it can be stored for future use by rolling it up and placing it in a PVC pipe. Clients who purchase billboards usually frame them and display them on a wall.

7

Displaying a Billboard In a Home

My brother Michael Littlefield chose to glue his 1950s Levi billboard on the wall of his family room, right over the door. It really adds a unique form of western art to the room.

Displaying a Billboard in a Flea Market or Antique Shop

Flea markets and antique shops are a great place to display these colorful ads. I had several displayed at the Pay N Pack flea market in north Portland, Oregon. Customers really enjoyed viewing the billboards that advertised War Bonds, Union 76, and a 1951 Chevrolet.

Displaying a Billboard in an Antique Mall

Some buyers such as Nostalgic Antiques in Gresham, Oregon added a framed border and spotlights to make this 1954 Studebaker ad look like an authentic outdoor billboard.

Displaying a Billboard in a Restaurant

Latte DA Espresso in the Hyde Park suburb in Boise, Idaho, displays a 1950s Ford billboard on one of their restaurant walls. This billboard accentuates their 1950s nostalgic theme.

Vintage car collectors with one or more cars housed in large buildings have billboards displayed on walls above there collections. Many vintage car buffs also collect gas and oil memorabilia and enjoy recreating the look of and old gas station. Car, gas, and oil ads are often displayed among vintage service station porcelain signs and other car collectibles.

Variety of Billboard Buyers

I have sold several billboards to many different movie studios. Recently three billboards were seen in the movie "Ray." The most prominent was an Eisenhower/Nixon election ad from 1952. Another ad for the U.S. Navy was featured in the movie "Men of Honor." The General Motors Museum in Michigan purchased a 1956 Cadillac Sedan de Ville ad, as well as a rare 1957 Chevrolet Cameo truck sign. Several individuals and restaurants including Ruby's Diner and Logan's Roadhouse have also purchased billboards from us.

Price Guide

The price guide included with the photos you will be viewing is based mainly on my own collection. I have seen a few other billboards, but not enough to do an extensive comparison. The lowest price is based on an ad in fairly good condition that may have some staining or tears. The higher price is for one in excellent condition.

Chapter Three
Billboards

Advertising

Advertising Council. "The Miracle of America," c.1960s. 8-1/2 ft x 19-1/2 ft. $1,000-1,900.

Appliances

Bendix-Automatic Home Laundry, c.1940s. 8-1/2 ft x 19-1/2 ft. $800-1,400.

Deepfreeze-Home Freezer, c.1940s. 8 ft x 19-1/2 ft. $1,100-2,300.

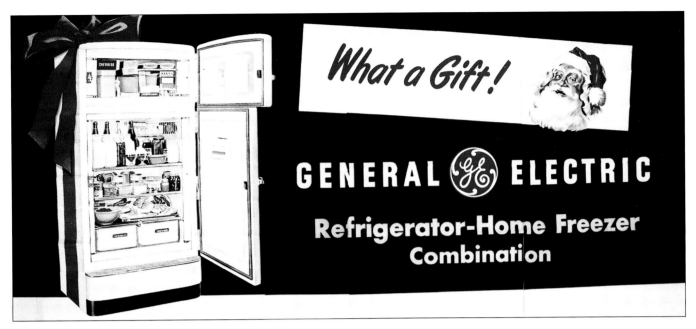

General Electric. "Refrigerator-Freezer Combination, c.1950s. 8-1/2 ft x 19-1/2 ft. $700-1,400.

General Electric. Automatic Washer, "Brightest, whitest wash in town," c.1950s. 7 ft x 19-1/2 ft. $800-1,400.

General Electric. Home Freezer, c.1950s. 8-1/2 ft x 19-1/2 ft. $1,000-1,800.

General Electric. Push-Button Range, c.1950s. 8-1/2 ft x 19-1/2 ft. $600-1,400.

Hotpoint. "Look to Hotpoint," c.1940s. 8-1/2 ft x 19-1/2 ft. $1,000-2,000.

Hotpoint. "Look! Pushbutton Cooking," c.1950s. 8-1/2 ft x 19-1/2 ft. $800-1,400.

Westinghouse. Laundromat, c.1940-50s. 7 ft x 19-1/2 ft. $900-1,800.

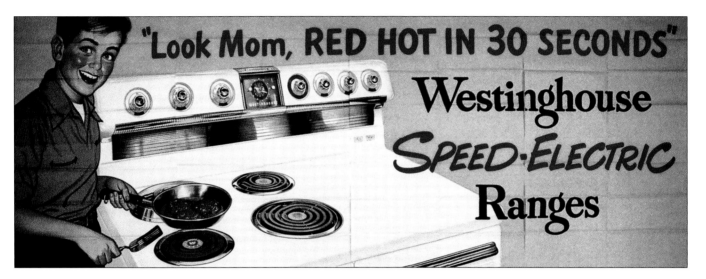

Westinghouse. Speed-Electric Ranges, c.1950s. 7 ft. x 19-1/2 ft. $1,000-1,800.

Zenith. America's Most Complete Appliance Line!" c.1946. 8-1/2 ft x 19-1/2 ft. $1,100-2,300.

Blitz. "The refreshing difference," c.1962. 9-1/2 ft x 20-1/2 ft. $1,200-2,300.

Blitz. "Guaranteed Satisfying Beer," c.1940s. 8-1/2 ft x 19-1/2 ft. $500-1,300.

Blitz. "Better Buy Blitz!" c.1950s. 8-1/2 ft x 19-1/2 ft. $800-1,700.

Budweiser. "They all want Budweiser," c.1950s. 8-1/2 ft x 19-1/2 ft. $1,200-2,600.

Budweiser. Democrat and Republican, c.1956. 8-1/2 ft x 19-1/2 ft. $1,500-2,300.

Budweiser. "Have lunch with us," c.1950s. 8-1/2 ft x 19-1/2 ft. $1,200-2,500.

Burgie. "Take a break," c.1940s. 8-1/2 ft x 19-1/2 ft. $1,200-2,600.

Hamm's. "Refreshing as the land of sky blue waters," c.1960. 8-1/2 ft x 19-1/2 ft. $400-1,500.

Hamm's. "In 'Stubbies,'" c.1960s. 8-1/2 ft x 19-1/2 ft. $900-1,900.

Hamm's. Steak and mug, "Refreshing as the land of sky blue waters," c.1960. 8-1/2 ft x 21-1/2 ft. $800-1,900.

Heidelberg. "Jumbo Quarts," c.1940s. 8-1/2 ft x 19-1/2 ft. $900-1,900.

Lucky Lager. "It's Lucky when you live in America," c.1950s. 8-1/2 ft x 19-1/2 ft. $800-1,800.

17

Lucky Lager. "Happy Holidays," c.1950s. 8-1/2 ft x 19-1/2 ft. $1,100-2,400.

Lucky Lager. "The Best Beer for You," c.1950s. 8-1/2 ft x 19-1/2 ft. $1,200-2,400.

Lucky Lager. You'll like Lucky, the aged beer," c.1950s. 8-1/2 ft x 19-1/2 ft. $1,200-2,300.

Lucky Lager. "Lucky Lager is always right!" c.1950s. 8-1/2 ft x 19-1/2 ft. $1,200-2,400.

Lucky Lager, c.1940s. 8-1/2 ft x 19-1/2 ft. $1,500-2,500.

Olympia. "It's the water," c.1950s. 9 ft x 19-1/2 ft. $800-1,900.

Olympia. "So refreshing," c.1950s. 9 ft x 19-1/2 ft. $1,200-2,300.

Olympia. "Always Welcome," c.1940s. 8-1/2 ft x 19-1/2 ft. $2,200-3,200.

Olympia. "Yours to enjoy," c.1950s. 8-1/2 ft x 19-1/2 ft. $1,200-2,300.

Schlitz. "Satisfies your thirst for something better," c.1950s. 8-1/2 ft x 19-1/2 ft. $1,100-2,400.

Schlitz. "If you like beer you'll love Schlitz," c.1950s. 8-1/2 ft x 19-1/2 ft. $1,200-2,200.

Schlitz. "Refreshing," c.1950s. 8-1/2 ft x 19-1/2 ft. $1,100-2,400.

Schlitz. "If you like beer…you'll love Schlitz," c.1950s. 8-1/2 ft x 19-1/2 ft. $1,200-2,400.

Sicks Select. "The famous beer from Seattle," c.1940s. 8-1/2 ft x 19-1/2 ft. $1,500-2,600.

Cadillac. The greatest Cadillac of all!" c.1956. 8-1/2 ft x 21-1/2 ft. $1,200-2,300.

Cadillac. "Writes its owner's biography!" c.1950s. 7 ft x 19-1/2 ft. $1,300-1,900.

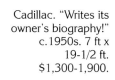
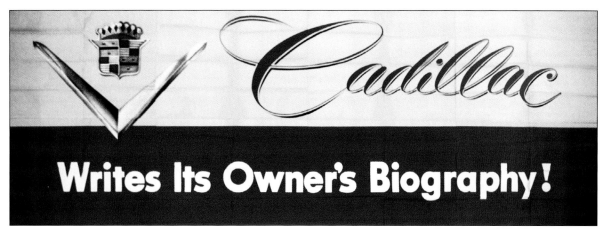

Chevrolet. "Brilliantly new for 1952!" c.1952. 8 ft x 19-1/2 ft. $1,400-2,300.

Chevrolet. "Youth, Beauty, Chevrolet, Action!" c.1956. 9-1/2 ft x 21 ft. $2,200-3,200.

Chevrolet. "Out-styles 'em all!" c.1955. 8 x 19-1/2 ft. $2,100-3,200.

Chevrolet. "All anyone could want!" c.1951. 8 ft x 19-1/2 ft. $1,500-2,300.

Chevrolet. First…and Finest…at Lowest Cost," c.1950. 8 ft x 19-1/2 ft. $1,200-2,400.

Chevrolet. "Handy dandy Chevrolet wagons!" c.1957. 8-1/2 ft x 19-1/2 ft. $1,400-2,600.

Chevrolet. "Pikes Peak Record Breaker!" c.1956. 9-1/2 ft x 21-1/2 ft. $1,600-3,100.

Chevrolet. "Just out and just wonderful! '57 Chevrolet," c.1957. 9-1/2 ft x 21-1/2 ft. $1,500-2,500.

Chevrolet. "Holds the whole team!" c.1956. 9-1/2 ft x 21-1/2 ft. $1,800-3,100.

Chevrolet. "Extra Values...exclusively yours," c.1949. 8 ft x 19-1/2 ft. $500-850.

Chevrolet. "Go '63 Chevrolet," c.1963. 9-1/2 ft x 21-1/2 ft. $1,400-2,300.

Chevrolet. "New 1951 Chevrolet," c.1951. 8 ft x 19-1/2 ft. $1,000-1,600.

Chevrolet. "New 1951 Chevrolet, Now on display," c.1951. 8 ft x 19-1/2 ft. $1,400-2,300.

Chevrolet. "For more and finer miles!" c.1951. 8 ft x 19-1/2 ft. $1,600-2,900.

Chevrolet. "Camaro by Chevrolet," c.1967. 9-1/2 ft x 21-1/2 ft. $1,700-3,100.

Chevrolet. "'Best dressed' car of 'the year," c.1955. 7-1/2 ft x 19 ft. $1,600-2,600.

Chevrolet. "Full of ginger...Jet-smooth Chevrolet," c.1962. 9-1/2 ft x 21-1/2 ft. $1,500-2,600.

Chevrolet. "Nowhere else such a big buy!" c.1954. 8 ft x 19-1/2 ft. $2,200-3,200.

Chevrolet. "Value that goes farther," c.1954. 8 ft x 19-1/2 ft. $1,500-2,300.

Chevrolet Truck. "New! Proved on the Alcan Highway!" c.1957. 9-1/2 ft x 21-1/2 ft. $2,100-3,100.

Chevrolet Truck. "Rugged and Reliable!" c.1953. 8 ft x 19-1/2 ft. $1,200-2,300.

Chrysler. "New Full-size Chrysler '62," c.1962. 8-1/2 ft x 19-1/2 ft. $1,200-2,300.

Chrysler. "Chrysler FirePower," c.1950s. 8 ft x 19-1/2 ft. $1,300-2,300.

DeSoto. "Fire Dome V-Eight," c.1950s. 8 ft x 19-1/2 ft. $1,200-2,000.

DeSoto. "Lets you drive without shifting," c.1949. 8 ft x 19-1/2 ft. $1,500-3,000.

DeSoto. "No other car rides like a DeSoto," c.1951. 8-1/2 ft x 19-1/2 ft. $1,300-2,300.

DeSoto. Arizona desert, "No other car rides like a DeSoto," c.1951. 9 ft x 20 ft. $1,500-2,600.

Dodge. "Elegance in action," c.1954. 8-1/2 ft x 19 ft. $1,300-2,300.

Dodge. "Power Packed Beauty," c.1953. 8 ft x 19-1/2 ft. $1,500-2,400.

Dodge. "Power Packed Beauty, New '53 Dodge V-Eight," c.1953. 8-1/2 ft x 19-1/2 ft. $1,400-2,300.

Dodge truck. "Ready for Business." c.1946. 8-1/2 ft x 19-1/2 ft. $1,500-2,300.

Ford. "Your family needs two Fords," c.1940s. 8-1/2 ft x 19-1/2 ft. $1,600-2,400.

Ford. "It's a bearcat!" c.1960s. 8-1/2 ft x 19-1/2 ft. $300-750.

Ford. "4 bedrooms, 3 baths…2 Fords," c.1956. 7-1/2 ft x 19 ft. $1,400-2,300.

Ford. "Real Thunderbird feel!" c.1963. 8-1/2 ft x 19-1/2 ft. $1,500-2,300.

Ford. "Here's your 52 Ford," c.1952. 8-1/2 ft x 19-1/2 ft. $1,400-2,400.

Ford. "Everybody's saying it: 'The '50 Ford's a hit!'" c.1950. 8-1/2 ft x 19-1/2 ft. $600-1,000.

Ford. "Only convertible that outsells Ford," c.1953. 8-1/2 ft x 19-1/2 ft. $600-1,200.

Ford. Falcon Ranchero, c.1960s. 8-1/2 ft x 19-1/2 ft. $1,400-2,600.

Ford. "Worth more for '54!" c.1954. 8-1/2 ft x 19-1/2 ft. $1,400-2,200.

Ford. "America's first choice in wagons," c.1955. 8-1/2 ft x 19-1/2 ft. $1,500-2,300.

Ford. "Glad we're a two Ford family!" c.1953. 8 ft x 19-1/2 ft. $1,200-1,800.

Ford. "It's a new kind of Ford for '57," c. 1957. 9-1/2 ft x 22 ft. $1,600-2,500.

Ford. "It's fun to go first," c.1956. 8 ft x 19-1/2 ft. $1,400-2,300.

Ford. "Keep ahead of winter with Ford Service," c.1960s. 8-1/2 ft x 19-1/2 ft. $800-2,200.

Ford. "Nothing newer in the world," c.1958. 8-1/2 ft x 19-1/2 ft. $1,600-2,500.

Ford. "Ford V-8 go like Thunderbird!" c.1950s. 7-1/2 ft x 19 ft. $650-1,100.

Ford. "Ford's economy twins for 1960," c.1960. 9 ft x 19-1/2 ft. $1,200-2,300.

Ford. "Trade in your troubles!" c.1960s. 7-1/2 ft x 19-1/2 ft. $1,500-2,800.

Ford. "Hottest thing going. 1969 Mustang," c.1969. 9-1/2 ft x 21-1/2 ft. $1,800-3,000.

Ford. "Merely terrific!" c.1953. 8-1/2 ft x 19-1/2 ft. $1,600-2,700.

Ford. "New Ford Victoria," c.1951. 8-1/2 ft x 19-1/2 ft. $1,400-2,500.

Ford parts. "You're right—they're right for Fords," (Kay Kiser), c.1950s. 8-1/2 ft 19-1/2 ft. $800-1,800.

Ford. 'Long, lean, and packed with punch," c.1957. 7-1/2 ft x 19-1/2 ft. $1,800-2,600.

Ford. "Best built body I ever ran into!" c.1957. 8-1/2 ft 19-1/2 ft. $800-1,400.

Ford. "Smooth getaway with Fordomatic," c.1954. 8 ft x 19-1/2 ft. $1,200-2,400.

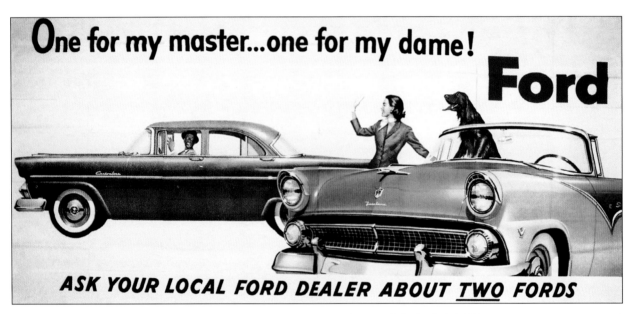

Ford. "One for my master...one for my dame!" c.1955. 8-1/2 ft x 19-1/2 ft. $1,600-2,500.

Ford. "More than ever...the standard for the American road!" c.1954. 8-1/2 ft x 19-1/2 ft. $1,400-2,400.

Ford. "The only wagon that outsells Ford station wagons," c.1957. 8-1/2 ft x 19-1/2 ft. $820-2,200.

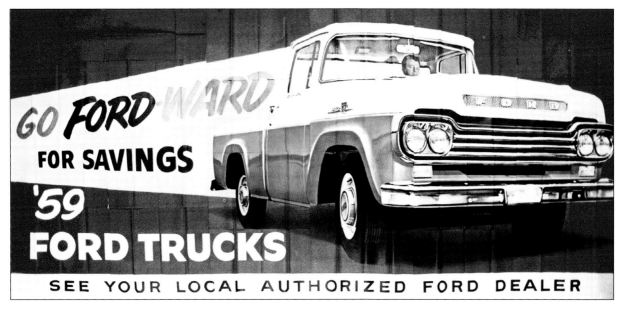

Ford truck. "Go Ford-Ward," c.1959. 9-1/2 ft x 20-1/2 ft. $1,400-2,300.

Ford truck. "…and brother, those Ford trucks save gas!" c.1954. 8-1/2 ft x 19-1/2 ft. $1,200-2,000.

Ford truck. "Most powerful pickup ever built!" c.1954. 8 ft x 19-1/2 ft. $1,500-2,300.

Ford truck. "Ford trucks last longer!" c.1950s. 8-1/2 ft x 19-1/2 ft. $1,200-2,100.

Ford truck. "Fordomatic drive!" c.1950. 8-1/2 ft x 19-1/2 ft. $1,400-2,400.

General Motors. "Any load-any road," c.1950s. 8-1/2 ft x 19-1/2 ft. $1,300-2,000.

Kaiser Henry J. "Save up to $600 a year!" c.1951. 8 ft x 19-1/2 ft. $1,800-2,700.

Mercury. "All over the map…it's Mercury!" c.1949. 8-1/2 ft x 19-1/2 ft. $2,200-3,000.

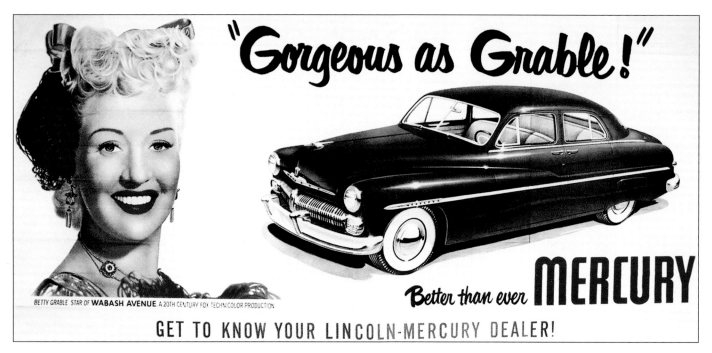

Mercury. "Gorgeous as Grable!" c.1950. 8-1/2 ft x 19-1/2 ft. $2,300-3,200.

Mercury. "Smooth as Bing!" c.1950. 8-1/2 ft x 19-1/2 ft. $2,400-3,200.

Mercury. "Comet fine car styling…compact car price," c.1960s. 9-1/2 ft x 20-1/2 ft. $1,600-2,300.

Mercury. "Mercury Cougar," c.1967. 9-1/2 ft x 21-1/2 ft. $1,800-3,000.

Mercury. "A winner like Wyman!" c.1950. 8-1/2 ft x 19-1/2 ft. $1,800-3,200.

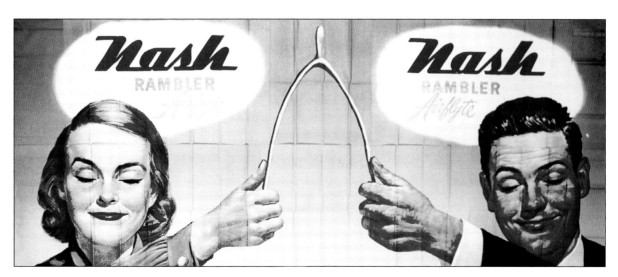

Nash. "Rambler Airflyte," c.1951. 8 x 19-1/2 ft. $800-1,600.

Nash. "C'mon–there's room for the whole troop!" c.1953. 8 ft x 19-1/2 ft. $1,200-1,600.

Nash. "Miss America says 'It's a sweetheart,'" c.1952. 8 ft x 19-1/2 ft. $1,500-2,400.

Nash. "Sure fun to drive!" c.1952. 8 ft x 19-1/2 ft. $1,000-1,600.

Nash. "Nash presents Farina's latest and greatest for 1954!" c.1954. 8-1/2 ft x 19-1/2 ft. $1,500-2,400.

Nash. "You see 'em everywhere!" c.1952. 8 ft x 19-1/2 ft. $900-1,600.

Nash. "Love at first Flyte," c.1950s. 8 ft x 19-1/2 ft. $1,200-2,000.

Nash. "Her master owns a Nash," c.1952. 8-1/2 ft x 19-1/2 ft. $1,000-1,600.

Nash. "Wind tunnel tests prove: 20% less air drag!" c.1949. 8 ft x 19-1/2 ft. $1,500-2,400.

Nash. "Frankly Sult…I'd trade this on a Nash," c.1951. 8 ft x 19-1/2 ft. $1,600-2,400.

Nash. "We're in Love with a Wonderful Buy," c.1950. 8 ft x 19-1/2 ft. $1,400-2,400.

Nash. "Rambler American," c.1961. 9-1/2 ft x 21-1/2 ft. $1,500-2,400.

Nash. "Now it's Dancer, Prancer, and Nash," c.1951. 8 ft x 19-1/2 ft. $1,400-2,400.

Nash. "New! 56 Nash V-8," c.1956. 8 ft x 19-1/2 ft. $1,500-2,400.

Nash. "I love your hair, eyes and your Dad's Nash," c.1950. 8 ft x 19-1/2 ft. $800-1,600.

Nash. "American Motors first new car! The '1955 Rambler," c.1955. 8-1/2 ft x 19-1/2 ft. $1,500-2,300.

Nash. "What won't they think of next," c.1951. 8 ft x 19-1/2 ft. $800-1,600.

Nash. "Brand new member of the Nash family! Rambler Airflyte Convertible Landau," c.1950s. 8 ft x 19-1/2 ft. $1,500-2,600.

Oldsmobile. "Time to take a 'holiday,'" c.1954. 8-1/2 ft x 19-1/2 ft. $1,400-2,400.

Oldsmobile. "Exclusively yours," c.1955. 8 ft x 19-1/2 ft. $1,900-2,700.

Oldsmobile. "Holiday for spring!" c.1953. 8 ft x 19-1/2 ft. $1,400-2,400.

Packard. "New, all-new Packard, the one for '51," c.1951. 8-1/2 ft x 19-1/2 ft. $1,400-2,600.

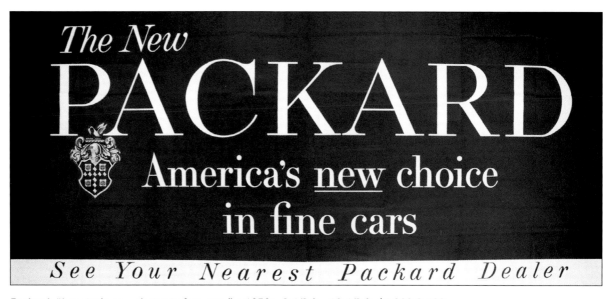

Packard. "America's new choice in fine cars," c.1950s. 8-1/2 ft x 19-1/2 ft. $1,200-2,400.

Packard. "Famous face–and what a figure!" c.1949. 8 ft x 19-1/2 ft. $2,200-3,000.

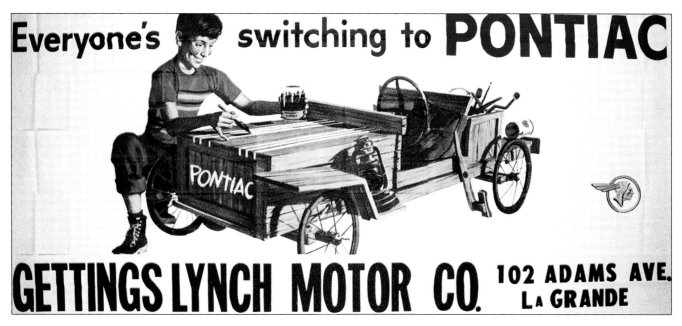

Pontiac. "Everyone's switching to Pontiac," c.1950s. 8 ft x 19-1/2 ft. $700-1,400.

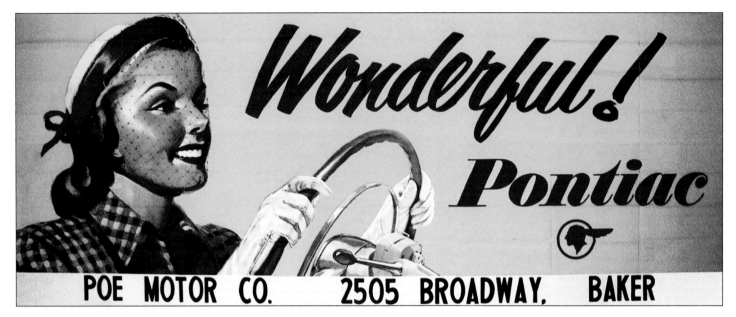

Pontiac. "Wonderful! Pontiac," c.1950s. 8 ft x 19-1/2 ft. $1,500-2,200.

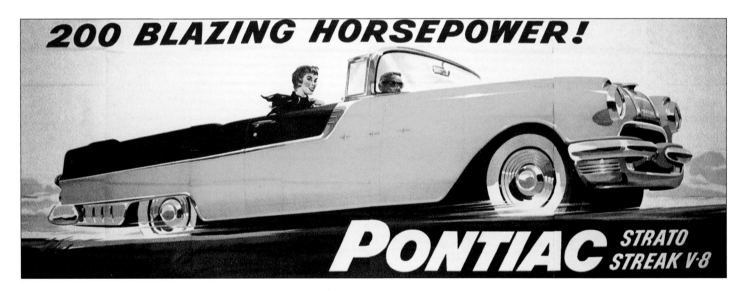

Pontiac. "200 blazing horsepower!" c.1955. 7 ft x 19 ft. $1,800-3,000.

Studebaker. "New 1953 Studebaker," c.1953. 8-1/2 ft x 19-1/2 ft. $1,400-2,400.

Willys. "Love at first ride," c.1950s. 8 ft x 19-1/2 ft. $1,300-2,400.

Willys. "Up to 35 miles per gallon!" c.1950s. 8 ft x 19-1/2 ft. $1,400-2,400.

Chainsaws

Remington. "More cutting power!" c.1950s. 8-1/2 ft x 19-1/2 ft. $400-1,200.

Charities

March Of Dimes. "You can help too!"
c.1940s. 8-1/2 ft x 19-1/2 ft. $900-1,700.

Red Cross. "Answer the call!" c.1953. 8-1/2 ft x
19-1/2 ft. $1,400-2,700.

Red Cross. "On the
job," c.1940s. 8-1/2 ft x
19-1/2 ft. $1,500-2,700.

Red Cross. "On the job...disaster relief," c.1940s. 8-1/2 ft x 19-1/2 ft. $1,400-2,700.

Catalina. "Around the world," c.1950s. 8-1/2 ft x 19-1/2 ft. $1,300-2,400.

Jantzen. "Gorgeous in
Jantzen," c.1950s.
8-1/2 ft x 19-1/2 ft.
$1,500-2,700.

Jantzen. "Swim suits
• sunclothes,"
c.1950s. 8-1/2 ft x
19-1/2 ft.
$1,500-2,700.

Levi's. "An old western custom," c.1950s. 8-1/2 ft x 19-1/2 ft. $1,400-2,700.

Levi's. "First in the west…because they last!" c.1950. 8-1/2 ft x 19-1/2 ft. $1,500-2,700.

Levi's. ."The West grew up in Levi's," c.1950s. 8-1/2 ft x 19-1/2 ft. $1,500-2,700.

Levi's. "Fit…For Action!" c.1950s. 8-1/2 ft x 19-1/2 ft. $1,400-2,700.

Levi's. "For rough going," c.1950s. 8-1/2 ft x 19-1/2 ft. $1,500-2,700.

Levi's. "Easier fittin' workin' or sittin'," c.1950s. 8-1/2 ft x 19-1/2 ft. $1,400-2,700.

Levi's. "As Western as the West itself, c.1950s. 8-1/2 ft x 19-1/2 ft. $1,400-2,700.

Levi's. "A cinch for longer wear," c.1949. 8-1/2 ft x 19-1/2 ft. $1,400-2,800.

Levi's. "The West's most famous brand," c.1950s. 8-1/2 ft x 19-1/2 ft. $1,200-2,600.

Levi's. "For solid comfort," c.1950s. 8-1/2 ft x 19-1/2 ft. $1,400-2,700.

The Cold War

Crusade for Freedom. "Help Truth fight Communism," c.1950s. 8-1/2 ft x 19-1/2 ft. $800-1,200.

Crusade for Freedom. "Your dollars do it!" c.1950s. 8-1/2 ft x 19-1/2 ft. $600-1,200.

Farming

Purina. "Sure pays off," c.1950s.
7 ft x 19-1/2 ft. $1,400-2,400.

Purina. "Their choice 2 to 1," c.1950s.
7 ft x 19-1/2 ft. $1,400-2,400.

Food

Arden. "Diced Cream,"
c.1940s. 8-1/2 ft x 19-1/2
ft. $1,000-1,700.

Brown & Haley. "Yankee Toffee,"
c.1947. 9 ft x 19-1/2 ft. $1,400-2,200.

Brown & Haley. "Quick lift. Mountain Bar!" c.1940s. 8-1/2 ft x 19-1/2 ft. $800-1,500.

Brown & Haley. "Taste treat ahead...Mountain Bar," c.1950s. 8-1/2 ft x 19-1/2 ft. $1,200-2,400.

Brown & Haley. "Almond Roca," c.1950s. 8-1/2 ft x 19-1/2 ft. $1,300-2,400.

Brown & Haley. "Overseas now...Home Soon. Mountain Bar, A Mountain of Goodness," c.1945. 8-1/2 ft x 19-1/2 ft. $1,400-2,600.

Brown & Haley. "She'll love Brown & Haley Chocolates," c.1950s. 8-1/2 ft x 19-1/2 ft. $1,500-2,500.

Brown & Haley. "Such good candy!" c.1950s. 8-1/2 ft x 19-1/2 ft. $1,600-2,400.

Brown & Haley. "She'll love Brown & Haley Chocolates," c.1950s. 8-1/2 ft x 19-1/2 ft. $1,500-2,400.

Brown & Haley. "It's a gift! Almond Roca1" c.1950s. 8-1/2 ft x 19-1/2 ft. $1,400-2,600.

Dennison's. "Home cooking in a can," c.1940s. 8-1/2 ft x 19-1/2 ft. $1,500-2,600.

Eddy's Bread. "No trick to treat!" c.1950s. 8-1/2 ft x 19-1/2 ft. $1,600-2,400.

Eddy's Bread. "Little league…big appetites," c.1950s. 8-1/2 ft x 19-1/2 ft. $1,500-2,400.

Eddy's Bread. "All hands agree," c.1950s. 8-1/2 ft x 19-1/2 ft. $1,400-2,400.

Eddy's Bread. "Really something extra," c.1950s. 8-1/2 ft x 19-1/2 ft. $1,500-2,600.

Hunts Catsup. "Deliciously yours," c.1960s. 8-1/2 ft x 19-1/2 ft. $1,100-1,700.

Hunts. Quality line, CHB Pickles, c.1950s. 8-1/2 ft x 19-1/2 ft. $1,200-2,000.

Boyd's Coffee. "Goes good anywhere!" c.1950s-60s. 8-1/2 ft x 19-1/2 ft. $600-1,100.

MJB Coffee. "Shake it! More measures– more flavor," c.1950s-60s. 8-1/2 ft x 19-1/2 ft. $700-1,400.

MJB Coffee. "Mmmm…More coffee flavor!" c.1960s. 8-1/2 ft x 19-1/2 ft. $600-1,400.

Nucoa. "The nutritious thrift spread," c.1950s-60s. 8-1/2 ft x 19-1/2 ft. $1,600-2,400.

Nucoa. "Rich in nutrition…rich in flavor," c.1940s. 8-1/2 ft x 19-1/2 ft. $1,700-2,600.

Nucoa. "Springtime flavor," c.1948. 8-1/2 ft x 19-1/2 ft. $1,700-2,400.

Nucoa. "So Good 'It melts in your mouth,'" c.1940s. 8-1/2 ft x 19-1/2 ft. $1,600-2,400.

Best Foods. "So smooth…," c.1950s. 8-1/2 ft x 19-1/2 ft. $1,100-1,800.

Aunt Jemima Pancakes. "Tempt Yo' Appetite Mornin', noon or night," c.1940s. 8-1/2 ft x 19-1/2 ft. $1,200-2,400.

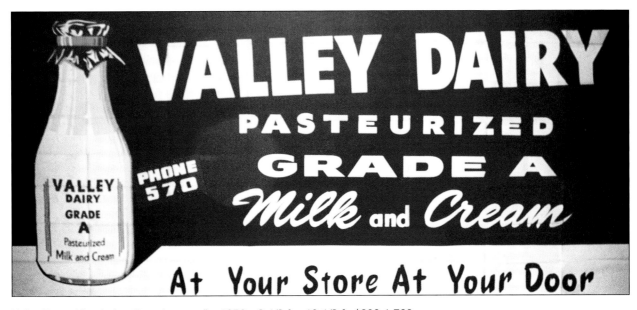

Valley Dairy. "Grade A milk and cream," c.1950s. 8-1/2 ft x 19-1/2 ft. $800-1,700.

Wrigley's. "Spear-mint Gum," c.1960s. 8-1/2 ft x 19-1/2 ft. $1,000-1,600.

Wrigley's. "Enjoy chewing delicious Juicy Fruit," c.1950s. 8-1/2 ft x 19-1/2 ft. $1,400-2,400.

Wrigley's. "Different-delicious Juicy Fruit," c.1960s. 8-1/2 ft x 19-1/2 ft. $800-1,600.

Gillette. "Change blades presto…easy shaves pronto!" c.1950s-60s. 8-1/2 ft x 19-1/2 ft. $800-1,500.

Sea & Ski. "Positively prevents sunburn," c.1950s. 8-1/2 ft x 19 ft. $600-1,200.

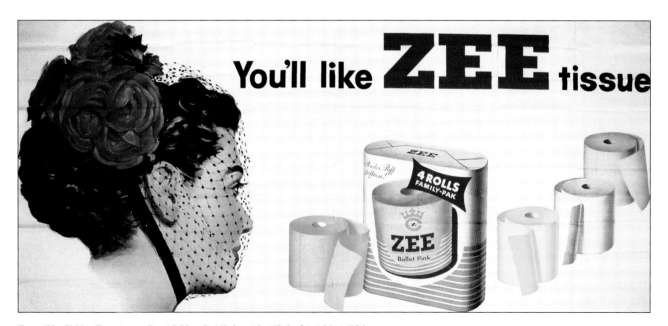

Zee. "You'll like Zee tissue," c.1960s. 8-1/2 ft x 19-1/2 ft. $1,100-1,700.

Insurance

OPS Insurance, c.1960s. 8-1/2 ft x 19-1/2 ft. $600-1,200.

Jewelry

Bulova. "For every gift occasion," c.1950s. 8-1/2 ft x 19-1/2 ft. $1,600-2,400.

Gruen. "Ring the bell with a Gruen," c.1950. 8-1/2 ft x 19-1/2 ft. $1,500-2,300.

Keepsake. "Your Keepsake…forever," c.1960s. 8-1/2 ft x 19-1/2 ft. $1,500-2,400.

Hermitage. "Enjoy the big H," c.1960s. 9-1/2 ft x 21-1/2 ft. $600-1,400.

Sunnybrook. "The light-hearted whiskey," c.1960s. 9-1/2 ft x 22 ft. $800-2,000.

Armed Forces. "America's finest women stand beside her finest men," c.1940-50s. 8-1/2 ft x 19-1/2 ft. $1,800-2,700.

Army. "To keep them safe," c.1940s. 8-1/2 ft x 19-1/2 ft. $2,000-3,200.

Marines. "O'er the ramparts they watch," c.1950s. 8-1/2 ft x 19-1/2 ft. $1,500-2,700.

Marines. "Join the Marines," c.1950s. 8-1/2 ft x 19-1/2 ft. $1,200-2,400.

Navy. "Travel, adventure with a future," c.1950s. 8-1/2 ft x 19-1/2 ft. $900-1,700.

Navy. "Fly with the fleet," c.1950s. 8-1/2 ft x 19-1/2 ft. $1,100-1,800.

Naval Reserve. "Only the finest serve in the Naval Reserve," c.1950s. 8-1/2 ft x 19-1/2 ft. $1,200-2,000.

Naval Reserve. "College Grads!…Serve as an officer," c.1950s. 8-1/2 ft x 19-1/2 ft. $1,200-2,000.

Miscellaneous

Dupont, Zerex-anti-freeze, c.1950s. 8-1/2 ft x 19-1/2 ft. $1,200-2,000.

Dupont. "Zerex…protects better," c.1950s. 8-1/2 ft x 19-1/2 ft. $500-1,000.

Evinrude. "Performance out of this world," c.1958. 8-1/2 ft x 19-1/2 ft. $1,200-2,400.

Movie theatre. "It's Movietime U.S.A," c.1960s. 8-1/2 ft x 19-1/2 ft. $800-1,500.

Old Trail Drive-in Theatre. "Pleasure bound!" c.1950s. 8-1/2 ft x 19-1/2 ft. $900-1,600.

RCA. "RCA Victor 45," c.1950s. 7 ft x 19-1/2 ft. $1,800-2,800.

Rodeo. "Frontier Days- Walla Walla, Washington," c.1950s. 8-1/2 ft x 19-1/2 ft. $1,200-2,200.

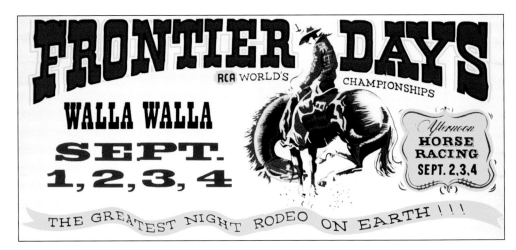

Simmons Beautyrest. "Body-fitting comfort head to toe, c.1960s. 9-1/2 ft x 22 ft. $1,100-2,400.

Nursing

Nursing. "Enroll as a Student Nurse," c.1960s. 8-1/2 ft x 19-1/2 ft. $700-1,600.

Conoco. "Conoco Super Gasoline with TCP," c.1950s. 8-1/2 ft x 19-1/2 ft. $300-600.

Conoco. "Hottest brand going," c.1960s. 9-1/2 ft x 21-1/2 ft. $1,200-2,600.

Conoco. "Clean rest rooms," c.1950s. 8-1/2 ft x 19-1/2 ft. $1,100-2,000.

Conoco. "Conoco Power," c.1950-60s. 8-1/2 ft x 19-1/2 ft. $300-800.

Mobil. "Mobiloil would'a kept you going," c.1950. 8-1/2 ft x 19-1/2 ft. $800-1,600.

Mobil. "Pay him out of my Mobilgas savings!" c.1950s. 8-1/2 ft x 19-1/2 ft. $800-1,400.

Mobil. "Trips are fun again," c.1940s. 8-1/2 ft x 19-1/2 ft. $700-1,500.

Mobil. "Should'a got a Miracle-fold map!" c.1950. 8-1/2 ft x 19-1/2 ft. $600-1,400.

Phillips. "Stretch your mileage!" [ostrich]. 8-1/2 ft x 19-1/2 ft. $1,000-2,000.

Phillips. "Perfect start!" c.1940s. 8-1/2 ft x 19-1/2. $1,200-2,400.

Phillips. "It's OK mister!" c.1940s. 8-1/2 ft x 19 ft. $1,300-2,400.

Phillips. "It's performance that counts!" c.1950s. 8-1/2 ft x 19 ft. $1,400-2,300.

Phillips. "It's a pleasure to please you!" c.1950s. 8-1/2 ft x 19-1/2 ft. $1,200-2,000.

Phillips. "It's performance that counts," c.1950s. 8-1/2 ft x 19-1/2 ft. $800-1,500.

Phillips. "It's performance that counts! Flite-Fuel," c.1950s. 8-1/2 ft x 19-1/2 ft. $700-1,400.

Phillips. "Stretch your mileage!" [giraffe], 8-1/2 ft x 19-1/2 ft. $900-1,600.

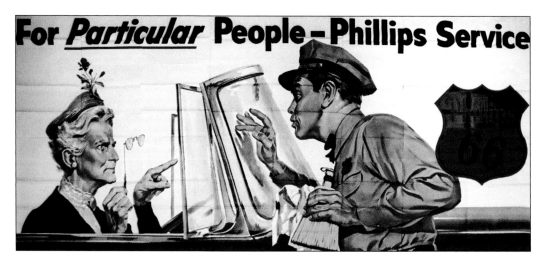

Phillips. "For particular people–Phillips Service," c.1950s. 8-1/2 ft x 19-1/2 ft. $1,400-2,300.

Phillips. "Drive right!" c.1950. 8-1/2 ft x 19-1/2 ft. $1,500-2,200.

Richfield. 'Years ahead" [spaceman], c.1950s. 8-1/2 ft x 19-1/2 ft. $1,800-2,700.

Richfield. "Partners in power," c.1950s. 8-1/2 ft x 19 ft. $1,700-2,700.

Richfield. "A great new refinery," c.1940s. 8-1/2 ft x 19-1/2 ft. $2,200-3,100.

Richfield. "Years ahead" [space station], c.1950s. 8-1/2 ft x 19-1/2 ft. $1,800-2,700.

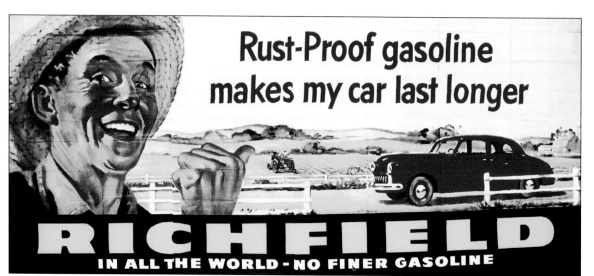

Richfield. "Rust-Proof gasoline makes my car last longer" [farmer], c.1940s. 8-1/2 ft x 19-1/2 ft. $1,300-2,600.

Richfield. "Years ahead" [men on the moon], c.1950s. 8-1/2 ft x 19-1/2 ft. $1,200-2,700.

Richfield. "If it's Richfield it's right," c.1952. 8-1/2 ft x 19-1/2. $1,000-1,800.

Richfield. "Rust-Proof gasoline makes our car last longer," c.1950s. 8-1/2 ft x 19-1/2 ft. $1,300-2,400.

Richfield. "Years ahead" [rocket to the moon], c.1950s. 8-1/2 ft x 19-1/2 ft. $1,500-2,700.

Richfield. "Planned to serve you," c.1950s. 9 ft x 19-1/2 ft. $1,600-2,800.

Richfield. "Years ahead" [rocket ship], c.1950s. 8-1/2 ft x 19-1/2 ft. $1,200-2,700.

Richfield, Disneyland ad, c.1950s. 8-1/2 ft x 19 ft. $1,000-2,300.

Shell. "The most powerful gasoline you car can use!" [hanging sign], c.1950s. 8-1/2 ft x 19-1/2 ft. $900-1,800.

Shell. "The most powerful gasoline you car can use!" [attendant], c.1950s. 8-1/2 ft x 19-1/2 ft. $800-1,600.

Shell. "Powerful good service, too," c.1950s. 8-1/2 ft x 19-1/2 ft. $1,400-2,500.

Signal. "Next time go farther with Signal Gas" [fire truck], c.1950s. 8-1/2 ft x 19-1/2 ft. $1,000-1,800.

Signal. "Most older cars…many '59s can save with Signal gas," c.1959. 9-1/2 ft x 20 ft. $900-2,000.

Signal. "Next time go farther with Signal Gas" [lady with roller skates], c.1950s. 8-1/2 ft x 19-1/2 ft. $900-1,800.

Signal. "Jet like action!"
c.1960s. 10 ft x 20 ft.
$1,000-2,000.

Signal. "Next time go farther with Signal Gas" [train engineer], c.1950s. 8-1/2 ft x 19-1/2 ft. $1,200-1,900.

Signal. "Out west this is the brand," c.1960s. 10 ft x 21 ft. $1,300-2,400.

Signal. "Next time go farther with Signal Gas" [policeman & lady], c.1950s. 8-1/2 ft x 19-1/2 ft. $1,100-1,800.

Signal. "Good signs to look for," c.1950-60s. 9-1/2 ft x 21-1/2 ft. $1,200-1,700.

Signal. "Next time go farther with Signal Gas" [fishing trip], c.1950s. 8-1/2 ft x 19-1/2 ft. $1,000-1,800.

Signal. "Be smart…and go farther," c.1960s. 9-1/2 ft x 21-1/2 ft. $1,200-2,200.

Signal. "More people go farther with Signal–than anybody!" c.1950-60s. 9-1/2 ft x 21-1/2 ft. $1,100-2,000.

Signal. "The best one for the road," c.1950s. 9-1/2 ft x 21-1/2 ft. $1,300-2,200.

Standard-Chevron, family outing, c.1950s. 8-1/2 ft x 19-1/2 ft. $1,200-2,400.

Standard-Chevron. "Safety you can trust…Atlas Tires," c.1940s. 8-1/2 ft x 19-1/2 ft. $1,600-2,400.

Standard-Chevron. "Puts spring in your driving," c.1950s. 8-1/2 ft x 19-1/2 ft. $1,300-2,300.

Standard-Chevron. "Wise man buy only octanes he need," c.1960s. 10 ft x 20 ft. $1,000-2,000.

Standard-Chevron. "Extra clean for fussy folks!" c.1950s. 8-1/2 ft x 19-1/2 ft. $1,400-2,400.

Standard-Chevron. "For the car you love," c.1950s. 8-1/2 ft x 19-1/2 ft. $1,300-2,400.

Standard-Chevron. "Our grease guns never miss!" c.1950s. 8-1/2 ft x 19-1/2 ft. $1,200-2,400.

Standard-Chevron. "Did you say Doubles engine life?" [boys in cars], c.1950s. 8-1/2 ft x 19-1/2 ft. $1,400-2,500.

Standard. "Did you say Doubles engine life?" [baseball player], c.1950s. 8-1/2 ft x 19-1/2 ft. $1,300-2,500.

Standard-Chevron. "Even 'Back-seat drivers' approve," c.1950s. 8-1/2 ft x 19-1/2 ft. $1,500-2,600.

Standard-Chevron. "Sure cure for knock, Doc," c.1960s. 9-1/2 ft x 21-1/2 ft. $1,200-2,400.

Standard-Chevron. "They're quiet when we grease 'em!" c.1950s. 8-1/2 ft x 19-1/2 ft. $1,300-2,400.

Texaco. "Sky Chief packs punch!" c.1950s. 9 ft x 19-1/2 ft. $1,000-1,600.

Texaco. "Tower of Power," c.1950s. 8-1/2 ft x 19-1/2 ft. $900-1,700.

Texaco. "Something we ladies appreciate!" c.1950s. 8-1/2 ft x 19-1/2 ft. $1,200-1,800.

Tide Water-Flying A. "Extra protection–no extra cost" [lifeguard], c.1950s. 8-1/2 ft x 19-1/2 ft. $1,300-2,200.

Tide Water-Flying A. "Enjoy the thrill of Tiger Power," c.1950s. 9 ft x 19-1/2 ft. $900-1,500.

Tide Water-Veedol. "My Dad knows his oil," c.1950s. 8-1/2 ft x 19-1/2 ft. $1,300-2,300.

Tide Water-Flying A. "Extra Protection–no extra cost" [baseball], c.1950s. 8-1/2 ft x 19-1/2 ft. $900-1,800.

Tide Water-Flying A. "You're in good hands at Flying A," c.1960s. 9-1/2 ft x 21-1/2 ft. $1,400-2,700.

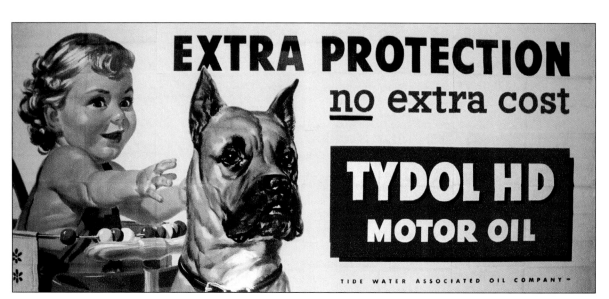

Tide Water-Flying A. "Extra Protection–no extra cost" [child and dog], c.1950s. 8-1/2 ft x 19-1/2 ft. $1,200-2,400.

library. We would like to keep you informed about other publications from Schiffer Books. Please return this card with your requests and comments. **(Please print clearly in ink.)**
Note: We don't share our mailing list with anyone.

Title of Book Purchased

☐ Purchased at: _____   ☐ received as a gift

Comments or ideas for books you would like to see us publish:

_____

_____

Your Name: _____

Address _____

City _____ State _____ Zip _____ Country _____

E-mail Address _____

Please provide your email address to receive announcements of new releases

☐ Please send me a **free** Schiffer Antiques, Collectibles, & the Arts
☐ Please send me a **free** Schiffer Woodcarving, Woodworking, and Crafts Catalog
☐ Please send me a **free** Schiffer Military, Aviation, and Automotive History Catalog
☐ Please send me a **free** Schiffer Lifestyle, Design, and Body, Mind, & Spirit Catalog

See our most current books on the web at **www.schifferbooks.com**
Contact us at: Phone: 610-593-1777; Fax: 610-593-2002; or E-mail: info@schifferbooks.com
SCHIFFER BOOKS ARE CURRENTLY AVAILABLE FROM YOUR BOOKSELLER

Printed in China

K:\user\do\wp\basic\boueeback

thousands of books in print,
fill out the back of this card
and return it today!

SCHIFFER PUBLISHING LTD
4880 LOWER VALLEY ROAD
ATGLEN, PA 19310-9717 USA

Tide Water-Flying A. "The first concentrated gasoline," c.1960s. 8-1/2 ft x 19-1/2 ft. $1,400-2,200.

Tide Water-Flying A. "Top performer with Tiger Power," c.1950s. 8-1/2 ft x 19-1/2 ft. $1,000-1,800.

Tide Water-Flying A. "Safeguard your motor," c.1950s. 8-1/2 ft x 19-1/2 ft. $1,200-2,100.

Tide Water-Flying A. "Get concentrated power with this cleanest gasoline," c.1950s. 8-1/2 ft x 19-1/2 ft. $1,300-2,000.

Tide Water-Flying A. "Surge over hills with Tiger Power," c.1950s. 8-1/2 ft x 19-1/2 ft. $1,300-2,100.

Union 76. "The finest" [model boat builder], c.1950s. 8-1/2 ft x 19-1/2 ft. $900-1,800.

Union 76. "The finest" [lady golfer & caddy], c.1950s. 8-1/2 ft x 19-1/2 ft. $1,200-1,800.

Union 76. "The finest, [polo player], c.1950s. 8-1/2 ft x 19-1/2 ft. $1,400-2,400.

Union 76. "The finest" [football fans], c.1950s. 8-1/2 ft x 19-1/2 ft. $1,100-1,900.

Union 76. "The finest" [woman sailor],c.1950s. 8-1/2 ft x 19-1/2 ft. $1,200-1,900.

Union 76. "The finest" [skiers], c.1950s. 8-1/2 ft x 19-1/2 ft. $1,200-1,900.

Union 76. "Union 7600 Oregon's finest gasoline," c.1950s. 8-1/2 ft x 19-1/2 ft. $1,400-2,300.

Union 76. "The finest" [the opera house], c.1950s. 8-1/2 ft x 19-1/2 ft. $1,200-1,700.

Union 76. "The finest" [lady shopper & chauffeur], c.1950s. 8-1/2 ft x 19-1/2 ft. $1,000-1,900.

Union 76. "The finest" [Cadillac], c.1950s. 8-1/2 ft x 19-1/2 ft. $1,400-2,400.

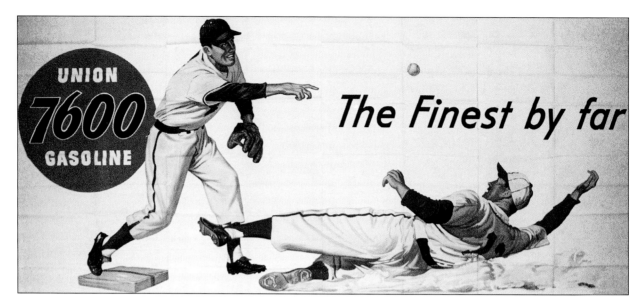

Union 76. "The finest by far" [baseball], c.1950s. 8-1/2 ft x 19-1/2 ft. $1,200-2,300.

Union 76. "The finest" [lady & yellow roses], c.1950s. 8-1/2 ft x 19-1/2 ft. $1,400-2,000.

Union 76. "The finest" [tennis players], c.1950s. 8-1/2 ft x 19-1/2 ft. $1,200-1,900.

Union 76. "The finest" [winning jockey & race horse], c.1950s. 8-1/2 ft x 19-1/2 ft. $1,400-1,900.

Union 76. "The finest" [sailboats], c.1950s. 8-1/2 ft x 19-1/2 ft. $1,300-1,900.

Union 76. "The finest…by far" [basketball], c.1950s. 8-1/2 ft x 19-1/2 ft. $1,200-1,900.

Union 76. "The finest" [beach resort couple], c.1950s. 8-1/2 ft x 19-1/2 ft. $1,400-2,000.

Union 76. "The finest" [fly caster], c.1950s. 8-1/2 ft x 19-1/2 ft. $1,300-1,700.

Union 76. "New Royal 76, please," c.1950s. 8-1/2 ft x 19-1/2 ft. $1,100-1,700.

Union 76. "The finest" [photographer & model], c.1950s. 8-1/2 ft x 19-1/2 ft. $1,200-1,700.

Union 76. "The finest" [woman & dog], c.1950s. 8-1/2 ft x 19-1/2 ft. $1,300-1-900.

Union 76. "The finest" [man & woman at opera], c.1950s. 8-1/2 ft x 19-1/2 ft. $1,400-2,400.

Union 76. "The finest" [golfers], c.1950s. 8-1/2 ft x 19-1/2 ft. $1,400-2,400.

Union 76. "The finest" [equestrians], c.1950s. 8-1/2 ft x 19-1/2 ft. $1,400-2,300.

Union 76. "Better engine protection!" c.1950s. 8-1/2 ft x 19-1/2 ft. $800-1,300.

Union 76. "The finest" [the wedding getaway], c.1950s. 8-1/2 ft x 19-1/2 ft. $1,300-2,300.

Union 76. "If it's service you want—see the Minute Men," c.1950s. 8-1/2 ft x 19-1/2 ft. $1,400-2,400.

Utoco. "Ladies love us," c.1950s. 8-1/2 ft x 19-1/2 ft. $1,100-1,700.

Utoco. "A great performer!" c.1950s. 8-1/2 ft x 19-1/2 ft. $1,200-2,400.

Utoco. "It's sure souped up!" c.1950s. 8-1/2 ft x 19-1/2 ft. $800-1,600.

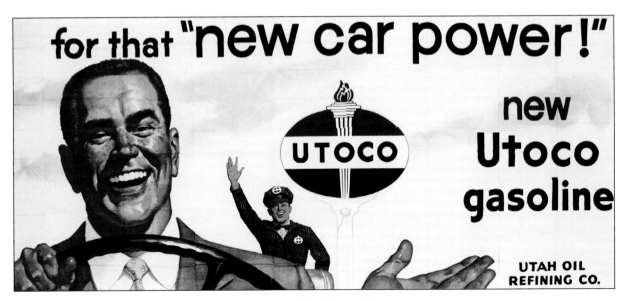

Utoco. "For that new car power!" c.1950s. 8-1/2 ft x 19-1/2 ft. $800-1,700.

Utoco. "4-wheel safety!" c.1950s. 8-1/2 ft x 19-1/2 ft. $1,200-2,300.

Utoco. "If you love your car change now!" c.1950s. 8-1/2 ft x 19-1/2 ft. $1,000-1,800.

Utoco. "Tops in performance," c.1950s. 8-1/2 ft x 19-1/2 ft. $1,300-2,400.

Fuller Paint. "They last…for home, farm, and industry," c.1950s. 8-1/2 ft x 19-1/2 ft. $1,200-2,300.

Fuller Paint. "For home…farm…industry…they last," c.1950s. 8-1/2 ft x 19-1/2 ft. $1,000-2,300.

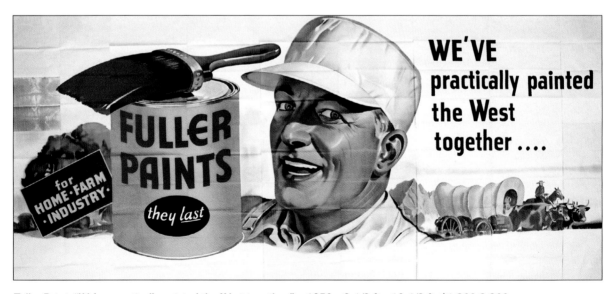

Fuller Paint. "We've practically painted the West together," c.1950s. 8-1/2 ft x 19-1/2 ft. $1,200-2,200.

Politics

Politics. "Ike and Dick…They're for you!" c.1952. 7 ft x 19-1/2 ft. $2,000-3,000.

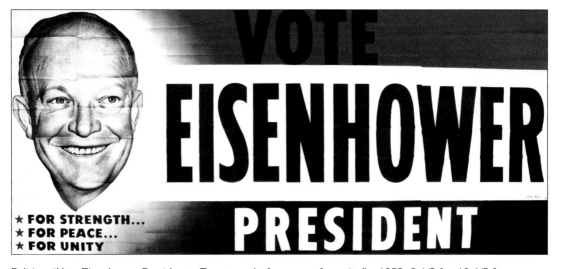

Politics. "Vote Eisenhower President…For strength, for peace, for unity," c.1952. 8-1/2 ft x 19-1/2 ft. $1,800-3,000.

Religion

Religion. "He restoreth your soul…Worship together this week," c.1950s. 8-1/2 ft x 19-1/2 ft. $200-900.

Red Goose. "Follow the Red Goose," c.1940s. 7 ft x 19-1/2 ft. $1,200-2,400.

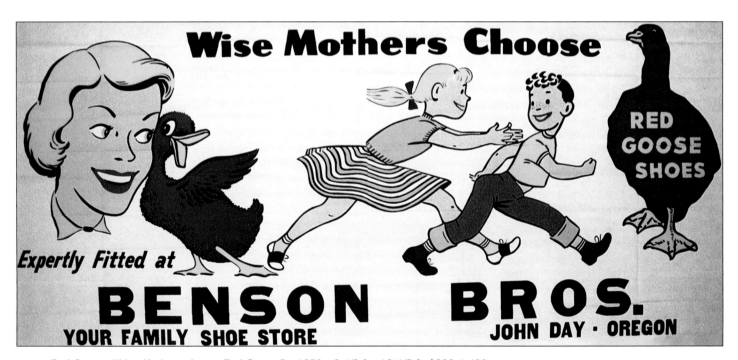

Red Goose. "Wise Mothers choose Red Goose," c.1950s. 8-1/2 ft x 19-1/2 ft. $800-1,400.

Remington. "Remington makes a powerful difference!" c.1950s. 8-1/2 ft x 19-1/2 ft. $1,400-2,200.

Winchester. "Power plus accuracy," c.1950s. 8-1/2 ft x 19-1/2 ft. $1,400-2,200.

Coca-Cola. "Every coke a fresh delight," c.1953. 8-1/2 ft x 19-1/2 ft. $1,200-2,300.

Coca-Cola. "Fresca," c.1967. 9-1/2 ft x 21-1/2 ft. $600-1,200.

Coca-Cola. "To lunch refreshed," c.1951. 8-1/2 ft x 19-1/2 ft. $1,400-2,700.

Coca-Cola. "You trust its quality," c.1953. 8-1/2 ft x 19-1/2 ft. $1,500-2,400.

Coca-Cola. "Great Serve," c.1957. 8-1/2 ft x 19-1/2 ft. $1,100-2,000.

Coca-Cola. "To drive refreshed" [woman beside car], c.1950s. 8-1/2 ft x 19-1/2 ft. $1,300-2,200.

Coca-Cola. "Work refreshed" [lineman], 8-1/2 ft x 19 ft, c.1950. $1,000-1,900.

Coca-Cola. "I'd love it," c.1953. 8-1/2 ft x 19 ft. $1,000-2,000.

Coca-Cola. "At home," c.1953. 8-1/2 ft x 19-1/2 ft. $1,300-2,000.

Coca-Cola. "For you," c.1951. 8-1/2 ft x 19-1/2 ft. $1,400-2,400.

Coca-Cola. "Play refreshed," c.1949. 8-1/2 ft x 19-1/2 ft. $1,200-2,300.

Coca-Cola. "For extra fun…take more than one!" c.1966. 9 ft x 21 ft. $900-1,600.

Coca-Cola. "For refreshment unequalled," c.1954. 8-1/2 ft x 19 ft. $1,200-2,000.

Coca-Cola. "My gift for thirst," c.1954. 8-1/2 ft x 19 ft. $1,400-2,700.

Coca-Cola, icicle cave, c.1949. 8-1/2 ft x 19-1/2 ft. $1,400-2,700.

Coca-Cola. "Brighten your meals with Coke," c.1955. 8-1/2 ft x 19-1/2 ft. $1,200-2,000.

Coca-Cola. "Shop refreshed," c.1950. 8-1/2 ft x 19-1/2 ft. $1,400-2,400.

Coca-Cola. "Drive refreshed" [woman driving convertible], 1940s. 8-1/2 ft x 19-1/2 ft. $1,300-2,300.

Coca-Cola. "Work refreshed"
[mechanic], c.1949. 8 ft x
19-1/2 ft. $1,400-2,700.

Coca-Cola. "Coca-Cola brings you Edgar Bergen with Charlie McCarthy," c.1949. 8-1/2 ft x 19 ft. $1,500-2,700.

Coca-Cola. "Travel refreshed," c.1949. 8-1/2 ft x 19 ft. $1,600-2,600.

Coca-Cola. "Vive la différence!" c.1956. 8-1/2 ft x 19 ft. $500-1,500.

Coca-Cola. "Me, too!" c.1952. 8-1/2 ft x 19 ft. $1,400-2,400.

Coca-Cola. "Quality you can trust," c.1951. 8-1/2 ft x 19 ft. $1,500-2,700.

Coca-Cola. "What you want is a Coke," c.1952. 8-1/2 ft x 19-1/2 ft. $1,500-2,600.

Coca-Cola. "Work refreshed" [judge], c.1949. 8-1/2 ft x 19 ft. $900-1,900.

Coca-Cola. "Friendliest drink on earth," c.1956 8-1/2 ft x 19-1/2 ft. $1,400-2,400.

Coca-Cola. "Now! King size too!" c.1955. 8-1/2 ft x 19-1/2 ft. $1,500-2,400.

Coca-Cola. "Large Coke! Zing!" c.1962. 8-1/2 ft x 19 ft. $300-700.

Coca-Cola. "Oh Mom… bring home Coke!" c.1957. 8-1/2 ft x 19 ft. $1,200-2,000.

Coca-Cola. "Hospitality," c.1950. 8-1/2 ft x 19-1/2 ft. $1,600-2,700.

Coca-Cola. "The frosty taste of Fresca. It's a blizzard," c.1967. 9-1/2 ft x 21-1/2 ft. $500-1,300.

Coca-Cola. "Hospitality in your hands," c.1949. 8-1/2 ft x 19-1/2 ft. $1,50-2,700.

Coca-Cola. "Things go better with Coke," c.1964. 9-1/2 ft x 21-1/2 ft. $400-1,100.

Coca-Cola. "Free decorations in Cartons of Coke," c.1966. 9-1/2 ft x 21-1/2 ft. $1,200-2,000.

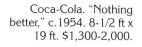

Coca-Cola. "Nothing better," c.1954. 8-1/2 ft x 19 ft. $1,300-2,000.

Coca-Cola. "Young man's fancy," c.1953. 8-1/2 ft x 19 ft. $1,400-2,000.

Coca-Cola. "To play refreshed" [swimmer], c.1951. 8-1/2 ft x 19-1/2 ft. $1,500-2,700.

Coca-Cola.
"Planning hospitality," c.1950.
8-1/2 ft x 19-1/2 ft.
$1,600-2,700.

Coca-Cola. "It's what folks want," c.1952. 8-1/2 ft x 19 ft. $1,400-2,600.

Coca-Cola. "Now! King Size too!" c.1955. 8-1/2 ft x 19 ft. $1,300-2,500.

Coca-Cola. "For Santa," c.1950. 8-1/2 ft x 19-1/2 ft. $1,300-3,000.

Coca-Cola. "Have a Coke," c.1952. 8-1/2 ft x 19-1/2 ft. $1,700-2,600.

Coca-Cola. "The frosty taste of Fresca. It's a blizzard!" c.1967. 9-1/2 ft x 21-1/2 ft. $900-1,600.

Coca-Cola. "Work refreshed" [office worker], c.1948. 8-1/2 ft x 19-1/2 ft. $1,400-2,700.

Coca-Cola. "Things go better with Coke" [Santa], c.1964. 9-1/2 ft x 21-1/2 ft. $1,600-2,400.

Coca-Cola. "Hospitality" [roses], c.1950. 8-1/2 ft x 19-1/2 ft. $1,400-2,700.

Coca-Cola. "The pause that refreshes" [roadster], c.1955. 8-1/2 ft x 19 ft. $1,400-2,400.

Coca-Cola. "Travel refreshed" [cowboy], c.1950. 8-1/2 ft x 19-1/2 ft. $1,200-2,400.

Coca-Cola. "Easy to take home," c.1947. 8-1/2 ft x 19-1/2 ft. $1,600-2,700.

Coca-Cola. "For the taste you never get tired of," c.1966. 9-1/2 ft x 21-1/2 ft. $500-1,000.

Coca-Cola. "Shop refreshed" [woman shopper], c.1949. 8-1/2 ft x 19-1/2 ft. $1,500-2,700.

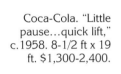

Coca-Cola. "Little pause…quick lift," c.1958. 8-1/2 ft x 19 ft. $1,300-2,400.

Coca-Cola. "The pause that refreshes" [Santa], c.1953. 8-1/2 ft x 19-1/2 ft. $1,600-2,700.

Coca-Cola. "Pause…King size!" c.1958. 8-1/2 ft x 19-1/2 ft. $1,400-2,400.

Coca-Cola. "Midsummer magic," c.1953. 8-1/2 ft x 19 ft. $1,500-2,700.

Coca-Cola. "What I want is a Coke," c.1952. 8-1/2 ft x 19-1/2 ft. $1,400-2,400.

Coca-Cola. "Shop refreshed" [lady with hat], c.1950. 8-1/2 ft x 19 ft. $1,200-2,400.

Coca-Cola. "Play refreshed" [roller skater], c.1950. 8-1/2 ft x 19-1/2 ft. $1,200-2,400.

Coca-Cola. "Good taste goes far," c.1958. 8-1/2 ft x 19-1/2 ft. $1,200-2,400.

Coca-Cola. "Now…Coke in king size too," c.1956. 8-1/2 ft x 19 ft. $1,400-2,400.

Coca-Cola. "Hospitality" [Santa], c.1948. 8-1/2 ft x 19-1/2 ft. $1.600-2,600.

Coca-Cola. "Thank you sirs!" c.1957. 8-1/2 ft x 19 ft. $1,200-2,400.

Coca-Cola, icicles and Coke bottle, c.1949. 8-1/2 ft x 19-1/2 ft. $1,400-2,700.

Coca-Cola. "Now! In 2 new sizes," c.1955. 8-1/2 ft x 19-1/2 ft. $1,300-2,700.

Coca-Cola. "Drive safely refreshed," c.1950s. 8-1/2 ft x 19-1/2 ft. $1,400-2,700.

Coca-Cola. "You trust its quality," c.1953. 8-1/2 ft x 19 ft. $1,300-2,400.

Coca-Cola. "Thirst asks nothing more," c.1952. 8-1/2 ft x 19 ft. $1,100-2,000.

Nesbitt. "All us big leaguers go for Nesbitt's," c.1950s. 8-1/2 ft x 19-1/2 ft. $400-1,200.

Royal Crown Cola. "The fresher refresher," c.1960s. 8-1/2 ft x 19-1/2 ft. $1,400-2,400.

Royal Crown Cola. "Think fresh!" c.1960s. 8-1/2 ft x 19-1/2 ft. $1,200-2,400.

States

Washington. "it's cool, it's green, it's great…Visit Washington State," c.1960s. 8-1/2 ft x 19-1/2 ft. $700-1,400.

General Tire. "Just keeps rolling along," c.1954. 8-1/2 ft x 19-1/2 ft. $1,200-2,000.

General Tires. "Straight to the point…top quality," c.1950s. 8-1/2 ft x 19-1/2 ft. $1,400-2,400.

General Tire. "Next time get Generals" [tortoise & hare], c.1950. 8-1/2 ft x 19 ft. $1,400-2,400.

General Tire. "Safest tire under the sun," c.1953. 7 ft x 19-1/2 ft. $1,500-2,400.

General Tire. "Give the kids a brake," c.1956. 7 ft x 19 ft. $1,300-2,400.

Kelly Tires. "Go worry-free in any weather," c.1950s. 7 ft x 19-1/2 ft. $1,200-2,400.

Kelly Tire. "Plenty of worry-free miles," c.1950s. 7 ft x 19-1/2 ft. $1,600-2,400.

Kelly Tire. "Know-how makes them better!" c.1950s. 7 ft x 19-1/2 ft. $1,300-2,400.

U.S Royal. "One ride proves the difference," c.1950s. 8-1/2 ft x 19-1/2 ft. $1,200-2,000.

Tobacco

Chesterfield. "So much milder..smells milder, smokes milder," c.1950s. 8-1/2 ft x 19-1/2 ft. $1,400-2,400.

Chesterfield. "Every smoker should smoke Chesterfield–much milder" [Arthur Godfrey], c.1950s. 8-1/2 ft x 19-1/2 ft. $1,400-2,800.

Chesterfield. "So much milder" [Rhonda Fleming], c.1950. 8-1/2 ft x 19-1/2 ft. $2,000-3000.

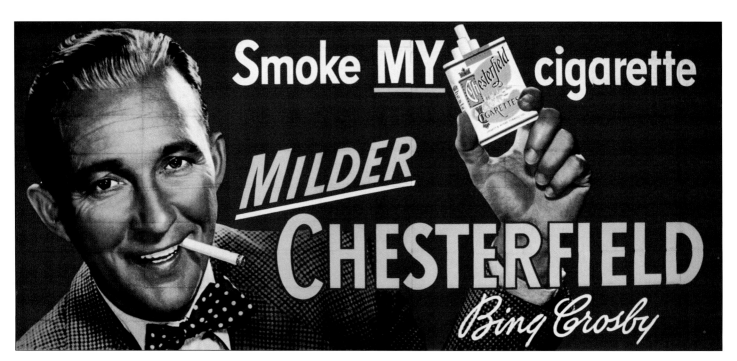

Chesterfield. "Smoke my cigarette" [Bing Crosby], c.1950s. 8-1/2 ft x 19-1/2 ft. $1,600-3,000.

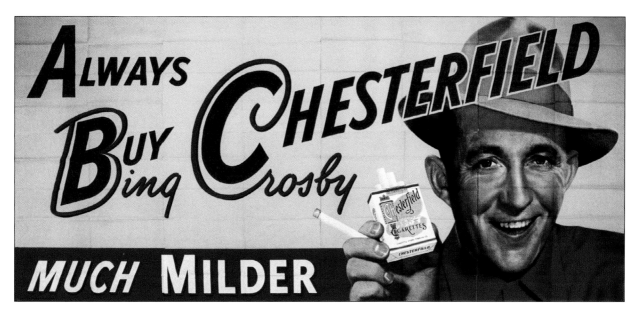

Chesterfield. "Always buy Chesterfield, Bing Crosby," c.1950s. 8-1/2 ft x 19-1/2 ft. $2,000-3,000.

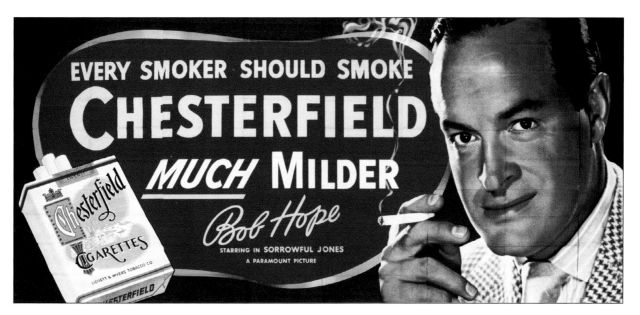

Chesterfield. "Every smoker should smoke Chesterfield" [Bob Hope], c.1950s. 8-1/2 ft x 19-1/2 ft. $2,000-3,000.

Copenhagen. "Makes the day worth while" [modelers] c.1954. 8-1/2 ft x 19-1/2 ft. $1,400-2,400.

Copenhagen. "The cheers are for Copenhagen," c.1945. 8-1/2 ft x 19-1/2 ft. $1,600-2,500.

Copenhagen. "Makes the day worth while" [hunter & dog], c.1954. 8-1/2 ft x 19-1/2 ft. $1,400-2,400.

Copenhagen. "Bank on Copenhagen," c.1945. 8-1/2 ft x 19-1/2 ft. $1,500-2,700.

Copenhagen. "Makes the day worth while" [fisherman], c.1954. 8-1/2 ft x 19-1/2 ft. $1,400-2,400.

Copenhagen. "It's a double pleasure!" 8-1/2 ft x 19-1/2 ft. $1,600-2,700.

Copenhagen. "Don't get caught without Copenhagen," c.1945. 8-1/2 ft x 19-1/2 ft. $1,400-2,600.

Kool. "Throat hot? Smoke Kool," c.1950s. 8-1/2 ft x 19-1/2 ft. $1,000-2,000.

Kool. "Got a cough? Smoke Kools," c.1950s. 8-1/2 ft x 19-1/2 ft. $1,200-2,000.

Marlboro. "Better makin's" [baseball player], c.1958. 8-1/2 ft x 19-1/2 ft. $1,100-1,700.

Marlboro. "Now in soft pack too!" c.1950s. 8-1/2 ft x 19-1/2 ft. $1,400-2,400.

Ford. "Power that Pur-r-r-s!" c.1950s. 7 ft x 19-1/2 ft. $1,400-2,400.

Ford. "Does more jobs…saves more hours." c.1949. 7 ft x 19-1/2 ft. $1,200-2,400.

Ford. "Built-in hydraulic power, c.1950s. 7 ft x 19-1/2 ft. $1,300-2,400.

Massey-Harris Pony. "The BIG small tractor," c.1950s. 8-1/2 ft x 19-1/2 ft. $1,400-2,400.

Massey-Harris. "Not much left for us crows!" c.1950s. 7 ft x 19-1/2 ft. $1,600-2,400.

Massey-Harris Combines, c.1950s. 8-1/2 ft x 19-1/2 ft. $1,200-2,300.

Massey-Harris. "Even I can't pull like that!" c.1950s. 8-1/2 ft x 19-1/2 ft. $1,200-2,400.

Massey-Harris Tractors. "5 power sizes–24 models," c.1950s. 8-1/2 ft x 19-1/2 ft. $1,300-2,400.

Massey-Harris. "Look... more good eating!" c.1950s. 7 ft x 19-1/2 ft. $1,200-2,200.

Massey-Harris. "For cleaner grain," c.1950s. 8-1/2 ft x 19-1/2 ft. $1,500-2,400.

Oliver. "Have you seen the new Oliver direct drive power take-off?" c.1940s. 7 ft x 19-1/2 ft. $1,600-2,400.

Oliver. "For a tough pull it's Oliver!" c.1940s. 7 ft x 19-1/2 ft. $1,400-2,400.

"Buy Savings Bonds for your country…and yourself, c.1940-50s. 8-1/2 ft x 19-1/2 ft. $1,200-2,400.

"Now let's all buy bonds," c.1940s. 8-1/2 ft x 19-1/2 ft. $1,400-2,400.